THE LITTLE

BURGER BIBLE

ZELLA EPPINGER

Bristol Publishing Enterprises
Hayward, California

A **nitty gritty**® Cookbook

Printed in the United States of America.

ISBN: 1-55867-282-6

Cover design: Frank J. Paredes
Cover photography: John A. Benson
Food stylist: Susan Devaty
Illustrator: Caryn Leschen

CONTENTS

BURGERS AND AMERICA

Ground meat has been around about as long as civilization and burgers have grown into a multibillion-dollar global industry: they are now a huge factor in the U.S. domestic gross national product.

J. Wellington Wimpy, a burger-obsessed character in the "Popeye" cartoon strip, did much to popularize hamburgers in America in the 1930s and '40s. From the 1950s on, tens of millions of Americans moving to the suburbs became barbecuers and took to burgers with glee.

By now, we Americans have had a long love affair with burgers. Consider these statistics:

- 96 percent of American households consume ground meats. Most of that is beef. Ground pork and turkey come next; then lamb. The remainder is venison, rabbit and even some ostrich and emu, which are also considered red meat.

- Three out of four American households have barbecue grills, and fifty-seven percent of all owners use them regardless of the season.

- Consumption of beef increases 25 percent over the Memorial Day weekend; over 7 percent of all beef eaten in the U.S is over the Fourth of July weekend.

Burgers have become so universal that the name has become generic, and so we have veggie burgers, tofu burgers, lamb burgers and sprout burgers. You'll find many of them in this book.

ABOUT GROUND MEAT

Ground meats have numerous benefits. Grinding tenderizes meat and allows even tougher, cheaper cuts to be more palatable. Grinding also exposes more meat surface area to heat and seasonings, causing it to cook more quickly and evenly and to be tastier.

You may have wondered what is the difference between "hamburger," "ground chuck," "ground beef" and "ground round."

- *Hamburger* is beef to which seasonings and beef fats may be added while the meat is being ground.
- *Ground beef,* however, is not permitted to have seasonings, extra fat, water, extenders or binders. The federal limit for fat is 30 percent by weight.
- *Ground chuck, ground round, ground sirloin,* refers to the cut of beef, not to fat content.

The rule followed by many supermarkets is that "regular" ground beef contains no more than 30 percent fat; "lean" no more than 23 percent; and "extra-lean" contains 15 percent fat or less. Extra-lean ground beef usually has a fat content between 4 and 7 percent.

If you can afford it, buy "natural," "grass-fed" or "free-range" beef, pork, lamb or poultry. Grass-fed meats are produced without commercial fertilizers and herbicides. Unlike most other commercially available meat products, they are not treated with any hormones or antibiotics. Grass-fed meats even have less calories than regular meats.

BURGERS AND HEALTHY EATING

According to U.S.D.A. nutritionists, a person with a daily requirement of 2,000 calories gets only 8 percent of those calories from a 3-oz. serving of ground beef, but receives 57 percent of protein, 34 percent of vitamin B12, 32 percent of zinc and 21 percent of phosphorus. In other words, ground beef burgers are low in calories but high in protein, vitamin B-12, zinc and phosphorus.

All meats, fish and fowl are high in protein, as are tofu and other soy products. Most meat burgers are also rich in B12, an essential vitamin sometimes lacking in the diets of non-meat-eaters.

There are many cooking techniques you can use to make your burgers healthier. The following suggestions reduce the possibility of carcinogens (HCAs) and reduce the saturated fat content of your cooked patties:

- For the healthiest, best-tasting burgers, cook them evenly over moderate heat (under 400°). This method brings meat sugars to the surface without burning them and enhances flavor.
- Flip your burgers on the grill frequently: this will keep them from charring and result in more even cooking.
- Foil placed under the patties prevents fat from dripping on the hot coals, flaming, and searing the patties.

- Onions and garlic, cooked either in or with burgers, contain sulfur, which impedes cancer. Both onions and garlic can also help to lower blood pressure.
- Mix in chopped, pitted sour cherries, plums, prunes, blueberries, seedless grapes, raisins or currants. Not only do burgers containing about 10 percent of these fruits gain a wonderful new taste, but they will be juicier, lower in fat and healthier for you.
- Microwave your burgers for a couple of minutes before barbecuing: this helps to promote even cooking.
- Make marinades containing low-sodium soy or tamari sauce, cider vinegar, lemon juice, Louisiana hot sauce, lemon juice or even green or black tea.
- Mix $1/2$ cup of textured soy protein per 1 pound of ground meat.
- Mix garlic, turmeric, rosemary or sage into marinades or into burger patties.
- Draining cooked-out fats and juices from your burgers can cut calories and fat content significantly. However, some fat serves to give burgers juiciness and flavor. Too lean a ground meat can be dry and crumbly and overcooks easily.

TIPS ON PREPARATION AND STORAGE

- Salt draws out moisture; try to use it only after cooking your burgers. Herbs, spices, capers and other seasonings are often good substitutes — and are healthier than salt.

- Be frugal when mixing meat with oatmeal, breadcrumbs, rice or other grain-based extenders. Too much of these grains makes burgers crumbly, and liable to burn.
- Ground red meats keep well in a refrigerator for three days, and in a freezer for up to six months. Turkey, chicken, or any fish or seafood will last in the fridge for only a couple of days; in the freezer for a month.
- Do not press or flatten burgers in the pan or on the grill — it makes them leathery. Nothing says a burger has to be round, either. Try shaping yours as triangles, squares, or whatever you prefer.
- Dip your hands in cold water before forming the patties. It prevents the meat from sticking to your hands.
- A small dent about 1/4-inch deep in the center of each side of a 1-inch-thick patty keeps a burger flat while cooking. This results in more even, healthier cooking and makes garnishes less likely to slide off.
  To guard against the possibility of food poisoning, always take the following precautions:
- Never thaw frozen foods uncovered or at room temperature. Always thaw them in the refrigerator or defrost in the microwave.
- Heat any processed or smoked meats to steaming hot and cook fresh red meats to an internal temperature of 160°, poultry to 180°. A good meat thermometer will do the trick. Keep

hot meats hot until you're ready to eat.

- Leftovers should be tightly covered and refrigerated within two hours after cooking — not two hours after you've finished dinner.
- Wash your hands in hot, soapy water for at least 20 seconds after handling raw meat. Also wash cutting boards, dishes, utensils and countertops in hot soapy water. After clean-up, dish cloths or sponges should be wrung dry and microwaved on high for 1 minute before reuse.
- Pay attention to expiration or "sell by" dates on any perishable food, particularly meat. If it's past expiration, don't buy it.

COOKING TIPS

I much prefer slow-cooked burgers of any variety. For one, this avoids charring the meat. Also, the longer cooking time allows flavors of different ingredients to merge and interact, providing better-tasting burgers.

On an outdoor gas or charcoal grill, I give thick beef or buffalo burgers sometimes as much as 30 minutes of total cooking time over low heat and will turn them 8 or 10 times. Lighter-textured meats such as lamb, pork and turkey don't require as much time or flipping.

If you prefer to use the broiler or skillet, brush patties with extra-virgin olive oil on the top before turning them on the grill. Brush them with oil again each time you turn them.

You can use canola oil as a substitute for extra-virgin olive oil. Canola oil is inexpensive, does not impart a distinct flavor and has many of the same health benefits as olive oil. Be aware of what oil you use: not all cooking oils are equally healthy.

GARNISH YOUR BURGERS WITH VARIETY

Onions, lettuce, tomatoes and pickles are the staple garnishes for burgers. But for a change, try varying your dishes with any of the following:

- Leeks, scallions and chives
- Raw mushroom slices, bell peppers or chile peppers (from the mildest to the hottest)
- Radishes, carrots, parsnips, cucumbers, eggplants, zucchinis, or any other of the huge family of squash
- Variations of lettuce and leafy greens, including endive, escarole, spinach, parsley, red and green cabbage and watercress
- Dill pickles, sweet pickles, relish, piccalilli, chutney, pickled chiles, artichoke hearts, horse-radish and any variety of olive

CHEESES 101

Almost any cheese will work beautifully with burgers. The fast-melting varieties — American,

Swiss, mozzarella, Monterey Jack, feta, Roquefort, Colby and mild cheddar — are best added to the top of the burger in the last minute of cooking.

Hard cheeses—Parmesan, Romano, extra-sharp cheddar—have fairly high melting points. Grating hard cheeses exposes more surface area to heat, causing them to melt more quickly. Also, grating gives you full flavor with less cheese.

SAUCING IT UP

Some commercial barbecue, chili and pasta sauces are very high in sugars and are very quick to burn. Read the list of ingredients on the label. If you are using a commercial sauce, dollop it on only after your burger is done cooking. That way, it won't have time to burn.

MARINADES

I began marinating because I thought it made the burgers tastier. Research now shows that marinades can have many other beneficial effects.

- Low-sodium soy sauce adds a unique flavor and functions as a powerful antioxidant and queller of carcinogens.
- Cider vinegar is an acid which stimulates enzyme action to tenderize meat and discourage bacteria.
- Lemon juice, another acid, imparts a tangy flavor to meat: its health effects are similar to those of cider vinegar.

- Tomato or vegetable juice are both acidic; both contribute flavor, potassium and lycopenes. I do not, however, recommend tomato-based barbecue sauces before or during grilling. These usually contain a lot of sugar and burn easily. If you do use them, do so only after the meat is removed from the grill.
- Italian salad dressing makes an excellent marinade. Try adding low-sodium soy sauce and/or Louisiana hot sauce.
- Dry red wine contains an unpronounceable something which allows the French to drink like fish and consume all manners of unwholesome fatty and sugary foods, all through a long and healthy life. If I can't fit a dry red wine into the chemistry of the marinade I'm trying to concoct, I take a glug or two for myself just on the general principle that 62.9 million French people can't be wrong.

Finally, the Guinness Book of Records says a record now of more than a dozen years' standing is that of a 5,520-pound burger fried in Seymour, Wisconsin in 1989.

The Seymourites claim their little burg is the home of the hamburger (as so do a whole lot of other places). In addition to slaughtering a small herd to produce the world's most prodigious burger, Seymour conducts a hamburger festival featuring events such as the 'Ketchup Slide.' Is this a great country, or what?

BEEF BURGERS

12	Spicy Beef and Bourbon Burger
13	Einstein's Beef and Vegetable Burger
14	All-American Beef and Pepper Burger
16	Aloha Burger with Guacamole and Pineapple
18	Blue Cheese Beef Burger
19	Bunless Mexican Burger
20	Burger Mignon Glace (Glazed Beef)
21	Beef Burger With Onions
22	Cheddar Burger Mignon
24	Capered Beef Burger
25	Cherry Beef Burger
26	Crunch-a-Bunch Beef Burger
27	Big Dilly Beef Garden Burger
28	Easy Spoon-On Beef Burger

SPICY BEEF AND BOURBON BURGER

This hearty recipe is rich enough for the end of a day's hunting or fishing.

1 cup finely chopped yellow onion
1 medium carrot, cut into matchsticks
1/2 cup canned stewed Mexican-style tomatoes
2 tbs. tomato paste
1/3 cup cider vinegar
1/4 cup brown sugar, packed
1 tsp. Worcestershire sauce
1 tsp. Louisiana hot sauce

1/8 tsp. cayenne pepper
1 tbs. black pepper
1 tsp. dried oregano
2 1/2 lb. ground sirloin
2/3 cup chopped yellow onion
1/4 cup bourbon
8 crusty hard rolls

In a large cast iron kettle or stockpot over low heat, combine onion, carrot, tomatoes, tomato paste, vinegar, sugar, Worcestershire, hot sauce, cayenne, black pepper and oregano. Cook uncovered, stirring occasionally, for 2 hours, or until thick. Cover kettle and keep warm.

In a large skillet over medium-high heat, cook meat and onions, breaking up meat with a spoon, until meat is pinkish-brown. Pour off and discard fat. Add meat mixture to sauce in kettle over low heat and cook for 1 hour. Stir in bourbon and cook for 10 minutes longer. Spoon onto split rolls.

EINSTEIN'S BEEF AND VEGETABLE BURGER

Servings: 8

The smartest thing about these burgers is that they taste wonderful and take only a few moments to prepare.

2 lb. lean ground beef
2 cups diced green bell pepper
1 cup minced yellow onion
½ tsp. minced garlic
2 cups thinly sliced fresh mushrooms
⅓ cup grated carrot

3 tbs. low-sodium soy sauce
1 tbs. Louisiana hot sauce
1 cup chopped fresh parsley
8 kaiser rolls, sliced and toasted
sliced tomatoes, sliced onion and sliced
   cheese for garnish

In a large bowl, combine beef with bell pepper, onion, garlic, mushrooms, carrot, soy sauce, hot sauce and parsley. Shape into 8 patties.

Heat grill to medium-low. Cook, flipping frequently, until patties are well browned and a meat thermometer shows internal temperature of 160°. Serve on toasted rolls; garnish with tomato, onion and cheese.

ALL-AMERICAN BEEF AND PEPPER BURGER

Ah, Norman Rockwell, where are you now that we need you to paint "The Beloved Burger," the only picture missing from your gallery of great Americana? You'll be nostalgic for these old-fashioned burgers even if you've just arrived from Mars.

SAUCE

1/3 cup finely chopped green bell pepper
1 tbs. dehydrated minced onion
1/3 cup chili sauce
1/2 cup mayonnaise

BURGERS

2 tbs. black pepper
2 lb. lean ground beef
3 tbs. extra-virgin olive oil, divided
6 slices Velveeta, cheddar, Swiss or Jack cheese
lettuce, sliced dill pickles, sliced tomato and sliced red onion for garnish
6 large crusty rolls, split

In a small bowl combine bell pepper, onion, chili sauce and mayonnaise. Cover and refrigerate.

In a large bowl, sprinkle black pepper over beef and mix well. Shape into 12 thin patties. brush each side with oil.

Heat grill to medium. Cook patties, flipping frequently, until patties are well browned and a meat thermometer shows internal temperature of 160°. Top 6 of the patties with cheese. Top with remaining 6 patties. Grill just until cheese is melted. Toast rolls on grill. Garnish with bell pepper sauce, lettuce, pickles, tomato and onion.

ALOHA BURGER WITH GUACAMOLE AND PINEAPPLE Servings: 4

Say "hello!" in your native tongue to these burgers that combine the cool taste of pineapple with the spicy zing of chiles, bedded in guacamole. And you'll want thick, crusty bread to handle the juicy contents.

GUACAMOLE

1 large avocado, mashed
1 large tomato, finely chopped
1/4 cup finely chopped red onion
1 tbs. fresh lemon juice with pulp
1/2 tsp. garlic salt
1 dash Tabasco sauce

BURGERS

1 tbs. canola oil
1 can (8 oz.) sliced pineapple in light syrup, drained, syrup reserved
1/4 tsp. ground cumin
1 lb. very lean ground beef
1/2 cup shredded sharp cheddar cheese
1 can (4 oz.) diced green medium chiles, drained
4 large hard rolls, split and toasted, or 8 slices sourdough, toasted

In a small bowl, combine all ingredients plus 1 tbs. of the reserved pineapple syrup. Cover and refrigerate.

In a skillet over medium-high heat, add oil and brown pineapple slices on both sides. Set aside. In a large bowl, blend 1 tbs. of the reserved syrup and cumin with beef and shape into 8 thin patties. Divide cheese and chiles evenly among 4 of the patties, leaving ½-inch margin all around. Top with remaining 4 patties. Seal edges well with fork or fingers.

Heat grill to medium. Cook patties, flipping frequently, until well browned and a meat thermometer shows internal temperature of 160°. Garnish with guacamole and pineapple slices and serve on rolls.

BLUE CHEESE BEEF BURGER

Remember those 1940s movies where everyone has a stiff upper-lip, and John Wayne shows up with a flamethrower in one hand, an automatic cannon in the other and a sneer on his lips? When he stops for lunch, this is what he has.

1 tbs. canola oil
2/3 cup finely chopped yellow onion
1 lb. ground chuck
1/3 cup dry breadcrumbs
2 tbs. dry white wine

1 small egg, well beaten
1/4 cup nonfat sour cream, divided
1/4 cup crumbled blue cheese
4 large English muffins, split
endive and sliced plum tomatoes for garnish

In a large skillet over medium-high heat, heat oil and cook onion until translucent. In a large bowl, combine onion, meat, breadcrumbs, wine, egg and 2 tbs. of the sour cream. Shape into 8 thin patties. Divide cheese evenly among 4 of the patties, leaving a 1/2-inch margin all around. Top with remaining 4 patties and seal edges well with fork or fingers.

Spray cold grill with nonstick cooking spray and heat to medium. Cook patties, flipping frequently, until well browned and a meat thermometer shows internal temperature of 160°.

Toast English muffins on grill. Garnish with remaining sour cream, endive and tomato.

BUNLESS MEXICAN BURGER

Servings: 6

These are otherwise known as tacos, a word which was first used as recently as 1934.

1 can (16 oz.) low-fat refried black beans
1½ lb. lean ground beef
2 tbs. dry taco seasoning mix
2 tbs. water
6 large taco shells
shredded lettuce, shredded sharp cheddar cheese, chopped onion, chopped tomatoes, minced
   jalapeño chiles and salsa for garnish

In a microwave-proof serving bowl, cover refried beans and microwave on high for about 4 minutes, stirring once. Set aside.

In a large skillet over medium-high heat, cook beef, breaking up with spoon, until browned. Put beef in a large strainer and rinse under very hot running water to remove fat. Return to skillet and add taco seasoning with 2 tbs. water. Reduce heat to low and simmer for 5 minutes, until thickened. Add beef mixture and refried beans to taco shells.

Garnish with lettuce, cheese, onion, tomato, jalapeños and salsa.

BURGER MIGNON GLACE (GLAZED BEEF)

In French, "glace" means "glazed." These glazed burgers have some of the classic taste of a filet mignon (little cut) steak.

1 lb. lean ground beef
4 strips lean bacon
3 tbs. honey
3 tbs. Worcestershire sauce
4 kaiser rolls, split
lettuce, sliced onion and sliced tomatoes for garnish

Shape beef into 4 patties. Wrap bacon slice around each patty and secure with toothpicks.

Heat grill to medium. Cook patties, flipping frequently, until well browned and a meat thermometer shows internal temperature of 160°.

In a small bowl, mix honey and Worcestershire sauce. Drizzle $1/2$ tbs. over each patty. Flip patties, drizzle remaining honey-Worcestershire mixture over each patty and grill for about 2 minutes longer, or until glaze begins to form.

Serve on rolls; garnish with lettuce, onion and tomato.

BEEF BURGER WITH ONIONS

This burger is as American as the Fourth of July. When you taste one though, it almost seems as if it should have a French name.

1 large red onion, chopped
1 cup dry red wine
1 tbs. extra-virgin olive oil
1 tsp. butter
1 lb. lean ground beef

¼ cup crumbled blue cheese, divided
1 tbs. extra-virgin olive oil
8 slices French bread
endive and thickly sliced Vidalia onion for garnish

In a food processor workbowl or blender container, puree red onion. In a small saucepan over medium-low heat, combine pureed onion, wine, oil and butter. Cook uncovered, stirring frequently, for about 30 minutes, until mixture is the consistency of jam. Set aside.

Shape beef into 8 thin patties. Divide cheese evenly among 4 of the patties, leaving a ½-inch margin all around. Spoon onion mixture over cheese. Top with remaining 4 patties, sealing edges well with fingers or fork. Brush each side with oil.

Heat grill to medium. Cook patties, flipping frequently, until well browned and meat thermometer shows internal temperature of 160°. Toast bread slices on grill. Garnish with endive and onion.

CHEDDAR BURGER MIGNON

This recipe is rich, tasty, and not particularly diet-conscious. Enjoy!

2 tbs. unsalted butter
3 green onions, including tops, finely chopped
1 clove garlic, minced
6 mushroom caps, thinly sliced
1½ cups freshly chopped parsley, divided
2 slices bacon
2 lb. lean ground sirloin
2 tbs. black pepper
½ cup country-style brown mustard, divided
¼ lb. extra-sharp cheddar cheese, shredded
4 crusty rolls, or 8 slices bread, toasted
sliced tomatoes, sliced dill pickles and olives for garnish

In a medium skillet over medium-high heat, melt butter and cook onions, garlic and mushrooms until onions are translucent. Transfer to a small bowl and add ¾ cup of the parsley.

In the same skillet over medium-high heat, cook bacon until crisp. Drain bacon on paper towels and crumble. In a large bowl, combine sirloin, pepper, ¼ cup of the mustard and remaining ¾ cup parsley. Shape into 8 thin patties. Divide mushroom mixture evenly among 4 of the patties, leaving a ½-inch margin all around. Spoon crumbled bacon, then cheese, evenly over top of mushroom mixture. Spread remaining ¼ cup mustard over remaining 4 patties. Place mustard-side down over cheese-covered patties and seal edges well with fork or fingers.

Spray cold grill with nonstick cooking spray and heat to medium-low. Cook patties, flipping frequently, until well browned and a meat thermometer shows internal temperature of 160°. Garnish with tomatoes, dill pickles and olives.

CAPERED BEEF BURGER

Capers grow on a prickly shrub that's been cultivated in the Mediterranean area for thousands of years. Its buds and young berries are pickled for seasonings or garnishes.

1 lb. ground chuck
2 tsp. small capers, drained
1 tbs. black pepper
1 tsp. dried oregano
1 tbs. canola oil
8 thick slices sourdough rye bread, toasted
sautéed onions for garnish

In a large bowl, combine meat, capers, pepper and oregano. Shape into 4 patties.

In a large skillet, add oil and cook patties over medium heat, flipping frequently, until well browned and a meat thermometer shows internal temperature of 160°. Garnish with sautéed onions.

CHERRY BEEF BURGER

Undercooked meat can harbor lethal bacteria, while well-done grilled meat can contain carcinogens. One solution? Add one part tart cherries to nine parts ground beef to reduce major carcinogens by 90 percent. Oh, lest we forget: cherry burgers are delicious.

1 lb. lean ground beef
2 oz. dried pitted cherries, finely chopped
2 tbs. low-sodium soy sauce
1 tbs. cider vinegar
1 tbs. black pepper
4 crusty rolls, or 8 slices bread

In a medium bowl, combine beef, cherries, soy sauce, vinegar and pepper. Shape into 4 patties.

Spray a cold grill with nonstick cooking spray and heat to medium. Cook patties, flipping frequently, until well browned and a meat thermometer shows internal temperature of 160°.

CRUNCH-A-BUNCH BEEF BURGER

Grape-Nuts and walnuts help give this burger its crunchy texture.

1 lb. lean ground beef
1/2 cup Grape-Nuts cereal, divided
1/2 cup chopped walnuts, divided
1 tbs. low-sodium soy sauce
1 cup shredded cheddar cheese, divided
1 tbs. black pepper

1 tbs. dried dill
2 tbs. extra-virgin olive oil
8 slices dark rye bread
thinly sliced red onion, sliced tomatoes and
    sliced cucumber for garnish

In a medium bowl, combine beef, 1/4 cup of the cereal, 1/4 cup of the walnuts, soy sauce, 2/3 cup of the cheese, pepper and dill. Shape mixture into 4 patties.

In a small bowl combine remaining cereal, walnuts and cheese. Set aside. Brush patties on each side with oil.

Heat grill to medium. Cook patties, flipping frequently, until well browned and meat thermometer shows internal temperature of 160°. Cover tops of patties with walnut-cheese mixture and grill until cheese melts. Toast bread slices on grill. Garnish with onion, tomato and cucumber.

BIG DILLY BEEF GARDEN BURGER

Dad loved Mother for many reasons, especially her hamburgers and dill pickles. Mother loved Dad and so she made thousands of each for him. This is my version of our family recipe.

1/2 cup sour cream
1/2 cup brown mustard
1/4 cup chopped fresh dill, packed
1 1/2 lb. lean ground beef
2 tbs. extra-virgin olive oil
4 hamburger rolls, split
sliced dill pickles, sliced tomatoes, sliced red onion and lettuce for garnish

In a large bowl, mix sour cream, mustard and dill. Set aside 1/2 cup of the mixture.

Mix beef with remaining sour cream mixture in a large bowl and shape into 4 patties. Brush each side with oil.

Heat grill to medium. Cook patties, flipping frequently, until well browned and a meat thermometer shows internal temperature of 160°.

Toast rolls on grill. Garnish with dill sauce, pickles, tomato, onion and lettuce.

EASY SPOON-ON BEEF BURGER

These are not the "sloppy joes" of your rash teen years ... even though there's a definite resemblance. You'll tell the difference with your first bite.

1 tsp. canola oil
1 cup finely chopped Vidalia onion
1 lb. lean ground beef
1 can (7 oz.) mushroom stems and pieces,
    drained

1 tbs. black pepper
4 croissants, split and toasted
fresh spinach and hickory smoke-flavored
    barbecue sauce for garnish

In a large skillet over medium-high heat, add oil and cook onion until translucent. Set aside.

In the same skillet, cook beef, breaking up with a spoon. Drain and discard fat. Reduce heat to low. Return onions to skillet with beef and add mushrooms and pepper. Combine well and cook for 7 to 8 minutes. Garnish with spinach and barbecue sauce.

CHIPOTLE, BACON AND SMOKED CHEESE BURGER Servings: 4

There's some fire in these burgers because of the chipotle peppers, but it's not hot enough to be alarming. The chipotles themselves and the bacon and cheese all contribute to the delightfully smoky flavor.

1 can (7 oz.) chipotle chiles in adobo sauce
2 tbs. sour cream
1 dash Liquid Smoke, optional
1 lb. lean ground beef
1 tbs. black pepper

4 strips lean bacon
4 slices smoked cheese
4 large whole wheat rolls, toasted
sliced tomatoes for garnish

Mince 3 of the chipotles. In a medium bowl, mix chipotles, 2 tbs. of the reserved adobo sauce, sour cream and Liquid Smoke, if using. Add beef and pepper and combine well. Shape into 4 patties. Wrap patties with bacon and secure with toothpicks.

Heat grill to medium. Cook patties, flipping frequently, until well browned and a meat thermometer shows interior temperature of 160°. Place cheese on patties to melt while burgers finish cooking. Garnish with tomato. Remind everyone to remove the toothpicks.

BEEF BURGER WITH SPINACH AND BELL PEPPER

Servings: 6

Here are burgers even the food police will applaud because of the amount of vitamins, minerals and other healthy stuff they contain. You also have permission to serve a nice red wine with them.

SAUCE

½ cup crumbled Roquefort cheese
3 tbs. mayonnaise
3 tbs. plain yogurt

1 tsp. black pepper
1 clove garlic, minced

BURGERS

¼ cup extra-virgin olive oil, divided
½ large yellow bell pepper, chopped
2 cloves garlic, chopped
1½ lb. lean ground beef
½ cup chopped fresh parsley
1 tsp. dried dill
2 tsp. black pepper

1 pkg. (10 oz.) frozen chopped spinach,
   thawed, squeezed dry
2 oz. tomato paste
1 large egg, lightly beaten
6 large kaiser rolls, split
sautéed Vidalia onion for garnish

Combine all sauce ingredients in a blender container or food processor workbowl and pulse 2 or 3 times until smooth. Place in a bowl, cover and refrigerate.

In a medium skillet over medium heat, heat 1 tbs. of the oil. Cook bell pepper and garlic, stirring frequently, for about 3 minutes, until tender. Place bell pepper mixture in a large bowl with beef, parsley, dill, black pepper, spinach, tomato paste and eggs and mix well. Shape into 6 patties. Brush each side with oil. Heat grill to medium.

Heat grill to medium. Cook patties, flipping frequently, until well browned and a meat thermometer shows internal temperature of 160°.

Toast rolls on grill. Garnish with sauce and sautéed onion.

GRECIAN BURGER WITH GARLICKY MAYONNAISE

Servings: 4

Greece is the birthplace of democracy, the Olympics and of Sophocles, Plato, Aristotle, Euripides and Aeschylus. Kalamata olives from Greece provide the final delicious touch to this dish.

SAUCE

2 tbs. mayonnaise
2 tbs. plain yogurt
1 clove garlic, minced

1 tsp. black pepper
1/2 cup crumbled feta cheese

BURGERS

1 lb. lean ground beef
1 large egg, lightly beaten
1/2 cup fine dry breadcrumbs
1 pkg. (10 oz.) spinach, thawed, squeezed dry
1 jar (2 oz.) diced pimientos
2 cloves garlic, minced

1/4 cup chopped fresh parsley
1 tsp. dried oregano
1 tsp. black pepper
4 large crusty hard rolls, split
pitted kalamata olives and sautéed onions for garnish

Combine all sauce ingredients in a blender container and pulse until smooth. Put in a small bowl, cover and refrigerate.

In a medium bowl, combine beef, egg, breadcrumbs, spinach, pimientos, garlic, parsley, oregano and pepper. Shape into 4 patties. Brush each side with oil.

Heat grill to medium-high. Cook patties, flipping frequently, until well browned and a meat thermometer shows internal temperature of 160°.

Toast rolls on grill. Garnish with sauce, olives and sautéed onions.

HEART OF BUTTER BEEF BURGER

Servings: 4

Let's suppose you, your loved one and a couple of friends plan a Sunday afternoon at the polo field, complete with a tailgater before the opening chukker. And let's suppose the regular cucumber sandwiches and caviar are a bit soggy. Here's the answer.

1/4 cup butter, softened
2 tbs. Roquefort cheese, softened
2 tbs. chopped fresh dill
2 tbs. chopped fresh parsley
1 clove garlic, minced

1 1/2 lb. lean ground beef
2 tbs. black pepper
4 large kaiser rolls, split
2 tbs. extra-virgin olive oil

In a small bowl, combine butter, cheese, dill, parsley and garlic. Place on plastic wrap and make a log about 1 1/4 inches in diameter. Place in freezer for at least 30 minutes.

In a medium bowl, combine beef and pepper. Shape into 8 thin patties. Cut frozen butter mixture into 4 equal pieces and place 1 piece in the center of each of 4 patties. Top with remaining patties, sealing edges well with fingers or fork. Brush each side with oil.

Heat grill to medium. Cook patties, flipping frequently, until well browned and a meat thermometer shows internal temperature of 160°. Toast rolls on grill.

SICILIAN BEEF BURGER WITH PINE NUTS & FONTINA
Servings: 4

All the ingredients for this great burger should be easy to find at your local grocery store.

1 tbs. chopped capers
2 tbs. grated Parmesan cheese
1/2 cup canned spinach, drained
1 tbs. toasted, chopped pine nuts
1/3 cup shredded fontina cheese

1 lb. lean ground beef
1 tsp. black pepper
1 tbs. soy sauce
1 tbs. extra-virgin olive oil
4 crusty rolls, split

In a small bowl, combine capers, Parmesan, spinach, pine nuts and fontina and mix well. Set aside.

In a medium bowl combine beef, pepper and soy sauce and shape into 8 thin patties. Divide cheese mixture evenly among 4 of the patties, leaving about 1/2 inch margin all around. Top with 4 remaining patties and seal edges well with fingers or fork. Brush each side with oil.

Heat grill to medium. Cook patties, flipping frequently, until burgers are well browned and a meat thermometer shows internal temperature of 160°. Toast rolls on grill.

BODY-BUILDER BEEF BURGER

The ingredients for these burgers are wholesome and healthy, especially the wheat germ.

1½ lb. lean ground beef
⅔ cup wheat germ
1 medium yellow onion, finely chopped
3 tbs. dry red wine
2 cloves garlic, minced
1 tsp. black pepper
2 tbs. extra-virgin olive oil
6 rye rolls, split and toasted
endive and sliced tomato for garnish

In a large bowl, combine beef, wheat germ, onion, wine, garlic and pepper. Shape into 6 patties. Brush each side with oil.

Heat grill to medium. Cook patties, flipping frequently, until well browned and a meat thermometer shows internal temperature of 160°.

Toast rolls on grill. Garnish with endive and tomato.

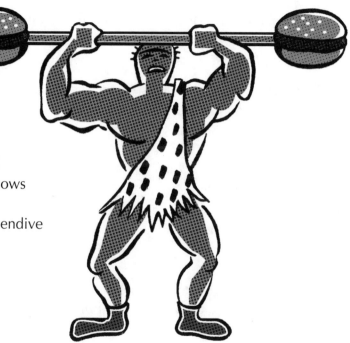

PICKLE-DILLY CIRCUS BEEF BURGER

I attended parochial school in a small town. There were always fund-raisers—most memorably, the summer hamburger fry and wienie roast. Fresh ingredients make this recipe a typical small town classic.

½ cup dill pickles, chopped and pressed dry between paper towels
½ cup finely chopped Vidalia onion
1 lb. lean ground beef
1 tbs. dried dill
4–5 dashes Tabasco sauce, or 1 tsp. black
  pepper
4 crusty hard rolls, split and toasted
sliced tomato, sliced onion and lettuce for
  garnish

In a medium bowl combine pickles, Vidalia onion, beef, dill and Tabasco. Shape into 4 patties.

Heat grill to medium. Cook patties, flipping several times, until well browned and a meat thermometer shows internal temperature of 160°.

Serve on toasted rolls. Garnish with tomato, onion and lettuce.

OPEN-FACE CHEESE MELT

Help! Your spouse's boss is arriving unexpectedly. Your pre-planned hamburgers are all that are possible. Fortunately, you have these cheese melts already underway. Boss is so enchanted that spouse is made executive vice president and you fly off to a second honeymoon.

2 lb. very lean ground beef
4 tbs. sharp brown mustard
$1/2$ lb. very lean bacon slices, halved
16 slices tomato-basil bread

8 slices low-fat Swiss cheese
alfalfa sprouts, sliced avocado, thinly sliced
onion and sliced tomatoes for garnish

Shape beef into 8 patties. Brush tops of patties with $1/2$ of the mustard. Top patties with bacon.

Heat grill to medium. Cook patties for 6 to 8 minutes, until bottom of patties are well browned. Remove bacon and set aside. Flip patties, brush with remaining mustard and top with reserved bacon.

Cook on grill until bacon is crisp and a meat thermometer shows internal temperature of 160°. Add cheese and grill until cheese melts. Toast bread on grill.

Garnish with sprouts, avocado, onion and tomato.

MIDWESTERN RUNZA BEEF BURGER

I don't know the origin of runza, but I suspect it may be German because the recipe comes from the Midwest where there are lots of people of German descent. A runza is a burger made with cabbage and onions and baked in a crust.

CRUST

1/4 cup warm water

1 pkg. dry yeast

2 tsp. sugar

3/4 cup scalded milk, divided

2 cups all-purpose flour

1/2 tsp. salt

BURGERS

1 lb. lean ground beef

3 cups finely shredded red or green cabbage

1/2 red onion, finely chopped

2 cups water

1 tsp. salt

In a medium bowl, stir in water, yeast, sugar and 2 tbs. of the milk. Let stand for 5 minutes, then add remaining milk, flour and salt and mix well. Turn onto a lightly floured board and knead until smooth and elastic. Transfer dough to a well-greased large bowl to rise for 1 hour or until doubled. Punch dough down and roll out into a 10 x 20-inch rectangle. Cut into eight 5-inch squares and refrigerate.

Heat oven to 350°. Brown beef in a large skillet over medium heat, breaking up meat with a spoon. Drain and discard fat. Reduce heat to low. Add cabbage, onion, water and salt and simmer uncovered, stirring occasionally, until liquid is gone.

Divide burger mixture equally among 4 squares of the dough, leaving a 1/2-inch margin all around. Top with remaining dough squares and seal edges well with fingers or fork. Let rise on greased cookie sheet for 10 minutes. Bake for 20 minutes. Flip runzas, then bake for 15 minutes longer.

BEEF PICANTE BURGER

I've been a spectator on a couple of trail drives where ranchers let their critters hoof it on the range. One day, a cowboy caught a rattlesnake and had it cooked up. I'd much prefer this simple and flavorful burger.

2 tbs. canola oil
1 medium green bell pepper, finely chopped
1 medium yellow onion, finely chopped
3 large stalks celery, tops included, finely
   chopped
2 lb. lean ground beef
2 tbs. black pepper
2tbs. dried sage

3 tbs. yellow mustard
1 tbs. cider vinegar
1 1/2 cups mild picante sauce
2 tbs. molasses
1 cup beef broth
24 slices sourdough rye bread, toasted
sliced tomatoes and sliced dill pickles for
   garnish

In a large skillet over medium-high heat, heat oil and cook bell pepper, onion and celery for 6 to 8 minutes, until onion is translucent. Add beef to skillet and cook, breaking meat up with a spoon, until pinkish-brown. Add black pepper, sage, mustard, vinegar, picante sauce, molasses and broth and simmer uncovered, stirring occasionally, for 20 minutes, until mixture is thickened but not dry. Spoon onto 12 slices of the rye bread. Garnish and cover with remaining bread slices.

MEXICAN BEEF BURGER

Here's an easy recipe for big, hefty burgers made of inexpensive ingredients on hand in every supermarket. Better yet, the recipe is easily multiplied to deal with almost any size of hungry crowd.

2 tbs. canola oil
1 lb. lean ground beef
1 can (14½ oz.) Mexican-style diced tomatoes
1 tbs. Worcestershire sauce
1 tbs. black pepper
1 tbs. coarse-ground brown mustard
1 tbs. chili powder

½ tsp. garlic powder
½ tsp. onion powder
½ tsp. brown sugar
8 large kaiser rolls, split and toasted
lettuce and shredded jalapeño Jack cheese for
    garnish

In a large skillet over medium heat, heat oil. Add beef and cook, breaking up with spoon, until pinkish-brown. Drain and discard fat. To beef in skillet add tomatoes, Worcestershire, pepper, mustard, chili, garlic powder, onion powder and sugar. Increase heat to medium-high and bring skillet contents to a boil. Reduce heat and simmer uncovered for 10 to 15 minutes, stirring occasionally, until thickened.

Spoon beef mixture onto halved rolls. Garnish with lettuce and cheese.

PORTOBELLO STACKED BURGER

The portobello is a very large mushroom of Italian ancestry, prized for its dense texture and meaty flavor. In this case, you want the biggest-possible portobellos, beefsteak tomatoes, Vidalia onion and a ripe but firm avocado.

4 large portobello mushrooms
1 lb. lean ground beef
½ cup chopped Swiss chard or spinach
½ cup crushed pretzels
¼ cup chopped fresh cilantro
1½ tbs. dry fajita or spicy taco seasoning
¼ cup extra-virgin olive oil
4 slices jalapeño Jack cheese
1 can (4 oz.) whole green chiles, drained
4 large crusty hard rolls, split and toasted
grilled onion, sliced tomato and sliced avocado for garnish

Cut off stems from mushrooms and trim and mince stems. Set caps aside. In a medium bowl, mix mushroom stems, beef, chard, pretzels, cilantro and seasoning. Shape into 4 patties, each the same size as mushroom caps. Brush patties on each side with oil.

Heat grill to medium. Cook patties, flipping frequently, until well browned and a meat thermometer shows internal temperature of 160°.

Split chiles in half lengthwise and discard seeds. Top patties with chiles and cheese and grill until cheese is melted. While patties are cooking, brush mushroom caps with oil and grill until browned on both sides. Top mushroom caps (gill-sides up) with patties.

Serve on toasted rolls, garnished with grilled onion, tomato and avocado.

SIMPLE APPLED BREAKFAST BURGER

Some credit for this must go to John Chapman (Johnny Appleseed), the legendary American character who wandered the midwest planting apple orchards in the 1800s. Enjoy these burgers at breakfast or brunch — or even lunch or dinner.

1 lb. ground sirloin
6 slices bacon, trimmed of most fat and diced
$\frac{1}{2}$ cup toasted breadcrumbs
$\frac{1}{2}$ tsp. ground allspice
$\frac{1}{2}$ tsp. dried thyme
$\frac{1}{2}$ tsp. cayenne pepper
$\frac{1}{2}$ tsp. onion powder
$\frac{1}{2}$ cup applesauce
1 tsp. cinnamon
6 croissants, split and toasted

In a large bowl, thoroughly mix all ingredients except croissants. Shape mixture into 6 patties. Heat grill to medium. Cook patties, flipping frequently, until well browned and a meat thermometer shows internal temperature of 160°. Serve on toasted croissants.

ZELLA'S MIXED GRILL BURGER

In England a mixed grill can consist of such oddments as a mutton chop, kidney, liver, bacon, sausage and tomatoes, all done to a leathery mystery. This is my own simpler, and more American variation in a burger.

4 Polish sausages, casings removed, halved lengthwise
4 slices smoked lean bacon, halved
1½ lb. lean ground beef
2 eggs, well beaten

½ cup burgundy or other dry red wine
1 envelope (1⅜ oz.) dry onion soup mix
1 envelope (1⅜ oz.) dry tomato soup mix
4 slices Swiss cheese, halved diagonally
4 crusty rolls, split and toasted

In a medium skillet over medium-high heat, cook sausages and bacon, flipping frequently, until cooked through. Drain and discard fat. Press sausages and bacon between paper towels to remove as much fat as possible.

In a medium bowl, combine beef, eggs, wine and onion and tomato soup mixes. Shape into 8 thin patties. Place 1 cheese half-slice, 2 sausage halves and 2 bacon strips on each of 4 patties. Top with remaining 4 cheese halves and remaining 4 patties. Seal edges well with fingers or fork.

Heat grill to medium. Cook patties, flipping frequently, until well browned and a meat thermometer shows internal temperature of 160°. Serve on toasted rolls.

PORK, BUFFALO AND OTHER MEATS

AS-PLAIN-AS-POSSIBLE BUFFALO BURGER

Servings: 4

Take one simple method, switch a few ingredients, and create endless variations on this theme. I don't think you can go through all the possible combinations in a lifetime, but if you do, let one of my grandchildren know.

1 lb. lean ground buffalo, lamb, venison, beef or veal
1 cup any shredded, grated or crumbled cheese
1 pkg. (1–1.5 oz.) dry salad dressing mix (ranch,
   Italian, Caesar, blue cheese or other)
4 rolls or 8 slices bread of choice, toasted
garnishes or toppings of choice

In a large bowl combine meat with cheese and salad dressing mix. Shape mixture into 4 patties.

Heat grill to medium. Cook patties, flipping frequently, until well browned and a meat thermometer shows internal temperature of 160°. Serve on toasted bread and garnish as desired.

BUFFALO, BACON AND BEER BURGER

Buffalo (or bison) meat is low in cholesterol and calories and extremely flavorful. Try serving these burgers with pork and beans on the side.

1 lb. ground buffalo
2 slices very lean bacon, diced
1/4 tsp. garlic powder
1/4 tsp. onion powder
1 tbs. black pepper
1/4 cup dark beer, room temperature
2 large eggs, well beaten

2 tbs. fresh lemon juice with pulp
1/2 cup finely crushed Grape-Nuts cereal
1 tbs. unsalted butter, melted
4 pita pocket breads
sliced tomato, thinly sliced green bell pepper
    and thinly sliced onion for garnish

In a large bowl, combine buffalo, bacon, garlic powder, onion powder, pepper, beer, eggs, lemon juice, cereal and butter. Shape into 4 patties.

Heat grill to medium. Cook patties, flipping frequently, until well browned and a meat thermometer shows internal temperature of 160°.

Lightly toast pita bread. Serve burgers in pockets and garnish with tomato, bell pepper and onion.

BURGER WITH A SPAMISH ACCENT

Servings: 6

Spam, a canned luncheon meat made from pork shoulder, has been around forever and millions of cans of Spam are sold each year. This change-of-pace burger helps to explain why.

1 tsp. extra-virgin olive oil
1 can (12 oz.) Spam, cut horizontally into 6 slices
Dijon mustard or mayonnaise, sliced Gruyere cheese, lettuce and sliced tomatoes for garnish
6 large crusty hard rolls, split and toasted

In a large skillet over medium-high heat, add oil and cook Spam until lightly browned on each side. Garnish with mustard or mayonnaise, cheese, lettuce and tomato and serve on toasted rolls.

CAMP SITE BUFFALO BURGER

Servings: 8

You've been captured by barbarians and carried off to the wilds. The chieftain comes back from the hunt with a huge buffalo slung over his hairy shoulder and grunts, "You cook now!" You decide to treat it like ground beef and here's how you become the co-chieftain.

3 tbs. extra-virgin olive oil, divided
1 large yellow onion, thinly sliced, separated into rings
4 small cloves garlic, minced, divided
1 medium-large turnip, grated
1/2 tsp. sea salt
2 lb. ground buffalo
1/2 cup Worcestershire sauce
1 tsp. red pepper flakes
8 crusty hard rolls, split
thinly sliced onion for garnish

In a large skillet over medium-high heat, place 1½ tbs. of the oil. Add onion and cook until translucent. Set aside.

In the same skillet, cook 2 cloves of the garlic for 30 seconds. Set aside.

In a small bowl, sprinkle turnip with salt. In a large bowl combine buffalo, Worcestershire sauce, pepper flakes and remaining garlic. Shape into 16 thin patties. Divide cooked garlic and turnip evenly among 8 of the patties. Top with cooked onion, leaving a ½ inch margin all round. Top with remaining 8 patties, sealing edges well with fingers or fork. Brush each side with oil.

Heat grill to medium. Cook patties, flipping frequently, until patties are well browned and a meat thermometer shows internal temperature of 160°. Toast rolls on grill. Garnish with onion.

CHORIZOS AND BEEF BURGER

Servings: 4

Chorizos are zippy sausages made of pork, garlic and powdered chiles. I love these burgers with a thick slices of tomato and onion.

2 chorizo sausages (about 2½ oz. each), casings removed, finely chopped
1 lb. lean ground beef
1 tbs. extra-virgin olive oil
4 crusty hard rolls, split and toasted
sliced tomatoes, sliced onion and endive for garnish

In a large bowl, combine chorizo and beef. Shape mixture into 4 patties.

In a large skillet over medium-high heat, add oil and cook patties, flipping frequently, until well browned and a meat thermometer shows internal temperature of 160°. Mop up pan drippings with rolls, cut-sides down. Garnish with tomato, onion and endive.

WET WEDNESDAY PORK BURGER

When the work week starts off badly on Monday and deteriorates rapidly from there, you need comfort, something to soothe your bruised soul and restore your weary body. Here's Doctor Zella's prescription.

1½ lb. lean ground pork
1 can (10½ oz.) condensed tomato soup, no water added
1 tbs. Worcestershire sauce
½ tsp. Louisiana hot sauce
½ cup finely chopped yellow onion
1 small carrot, shaved into thin ribbons
2 cups shredded cheddar cheese
6 large crusty hard rolls, split

In a large bowl mix pork, soup, sauces, onion and carrot. Shape into 6 patties.

Heat broiler and spray broiler pan with nonstick cooking spray. Arrange on broiling pan and cook about 6 inches from heat, flipping patties twice, until browned and a meat thermometer shows internal temperature of 150°. Sprinkle patties with cheese and broil until cheese melts.

ADOBO AND CHIPOTLE PORK BURGER

Servings: 8

A chipotle chile is a dried, smoked jalapeño chile. That doesn't dampen the fire in it. Adobo sauce consists of spicy seasonings, vinegar, onions and tomatoes. You may wish to use rubber gloves when preparing these hot chiles.

2 tbs. extra-virgin olive oil, divided
1 medium yellow onion, chopped
1 can (7 oz.) chipotle chiles in adobo sauce
2 lb. lean ground pork
2 eggs, lightly beaten
2 tbs. fine dry rye breadcrumbs
1/3 cup chopped fresh cilantro
1/2 tsp. honey
16 slices crusty rye bread, toasted
coarsely chopped avocados and sour cream for garnish

In a large skillet over medium heat, heat 1 tbs. of the oil and cook onion until translucent. Remove onion to a large bowl. Add 2 tbs. of the adobo sauce to bowl with onion. Seed and mince 3 of the chipotles and add to bowl. Add pork, eggs, breadcrumbs, cilantro and honey and mix well by hand. Shape mixture into 8 patties.

Return large skillet to stove over medium-high heat and add remaining 1 tbs. oil. Cook patties, flipping frequently, until well browned and a meat thermometer shows internal temperature of 160°. Garnish with avocados and sour cream.

HAWAIIAN-STYLE PORK OR LAMB BURGER

Servings: 6

There aren't many sheep in Hawaii, which may be why a pig is more usually cooked at luaus. However, for this burger, I also like to use lamb, as it blends well with the other ingredients.

2 lb. lean ground lamb
2/3 cup minced red bell pepper
1 tbs. grated lemon zest
2/3 tsp. ground ginger
1/3 cup low-sodium soy sauce

Large fresh pineapple, peeled and cut into 6
    slices each 1/2-inch thick
1/2 cup plain yogurt
2 tbs. extra-virgin olive oil
6 whole wheat rolls, split

In a large bowl, mix lamb, bell pepper, lemon zest, ginger and soy sauce. Shape into 12 thin patties. Trim pineapple slices to slightly smaller diameter than patties. Top each of 6 patties with pineapple slice. Dollop about 1 tbs. yogurt in center of each slice. Top with remaining 6 patties. Seal edges well with fingers or fork. Brush each side with oil.

Heat grill to medium. Cook patties, flipping frequently, until well browned and a meat thermometer shows internal temperature of 160°. Toast rolls on grill.

BUFFALO BURGER WITH TOMATILLOS, CILANTRO AND LIME

Servings: 6

Tomatillos, cilantro and lime give this burger a modern, slightly south-of-the-border flavor.

¼ lb. tomatillos, husked, rinsed and thinly sliced
1 large sweet onion, thinly sliced
⅓ cup fresh lime juice, including pulp
½ cup fresh orange juice, including pulp
1 cup chopped fresh cilantro

1 tbs. black pepper
1 tsp. red pepper flakes
1½ lb. ground buffalo
12 slices pesto bread or any bread
sharp stoneground mustard and escarole for garnish

In a medium bowl, mix tomatillos, onion, lime and orange juices, cilantro, pepper and pepper flakes. Set aside. Shape buffalo into 6 patties.

Heat grill to medium. Cook patties, flipping frequently, until well browned and a meat thermometer shows internal temperature of 160°. Toast bread on grill. Serve with tomatillo mixture and garnish with mustard and escarole.

BACON BEEF BURGER

The burgers themselves can made with beef, buffalo, venison or turkey; can be embellished with any cheese; and can be garnished with any type of greens, onions, tomatoes, or— for a taste surprise—thin slices of apples, radishes or even turnips.

8 strips lean bacon, divided
1½ lb. lean ground beef
2 tbs. low-sodium soy sauce
1–2 drops Liquid Smoke, optional
4 thin slices cheese, any kind
4 large crusty rolls, split

Cut 4 of the bacon strips in half. In a medium skillet over medium-high heat, cook bacon half-slices until crisp. Set aside on paper towels. In a medium bowl, combine meat, soy sauce and Liquid Smoke (if using) and shape into 4 patties. Wrap strip of reserved bacon around each patty; secure with toothpicks.

Heat grill to medium. Cook patties, flipping frequently, until well browned and a meat thermometer shows internal temperature of 160°. Place 2 pieces of reserved cooked bacon on each patty, cover with cheese and cook until cheese melts. Toast rolls on grill.

LAMB BURGERS

CORFU LAMB BURGER WITH CUCUMBER SAUCE

Servings: 6

The island of Corfu sits in the Ionian Sea near the border of Greece and Albania. This recipe, with its cucumber-yogurt sauce and herbs, evokes the beautiful landscape and climate of the region.

1/2 cup peeled, seeded and diced cucumber
1/2 cup plain yogurt
1 tbs. chopped fresh parsley
2 small cloves garlic, minced
Black pepper to taste
1/2 cup coarsely chopped fresh mint
1/2 cup finely chopped red onion
2 tbs. grated lemon zest

1 tbs. lemon juice
1/3 tsp. cayenne pepper
1 1/2 lb. lean ground lamb
1 pkg. (10 oz.) frozen chopped spinach, thawed and drained
3 cloves garlic, minced
3 tbs. extra-virgin olive oil
6 large caraway seed rolls, split

In a medium bowl, combine cucumber, yogurt, parsley, garlic and pepper to make sauce; cover and refrigerate.

In a large bowl, mix mint, onion, lemon zest, lemon juice, cayenne, lamb, spinach and garlic. Shape into 6 patties. Brush each side with oil.

Heat grill to medium. Cook patties, flipping frequently, until well browned and a meat thermometer shows internal temperature of 160°.

Toast rolls on grill. Garnish with cucumber sauce.

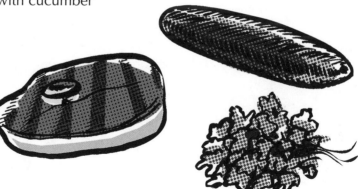

SAUCILY-MINTED LAMB BURGER

Lean ground pork tenderloin, ground turkey or chicken thigh meat would also work well in this recipe. However, lamb is traditional with mint, yogurt and pita.

1 large avocado, mashed
¾ cup plain yogurt
⅓ cup finely chopped fresh mint, divided
1 tsp. salt, divided
2 tsp. black pepper, divided

2 cloves garlic, minced, divided
1½ lb. lean ground lamb
2 tbs. extra-virgin olive oil
4 pita pocket breads
endive and thinly sliced red onion for garnish

In a small bowl, combine avocado with yogurt, half of the chopped mint, ½ tsp. of the salt, 1 tsp. of the pepper and 1 clove of the garlic. Cover and refrigerate.

In a medium bowl, mix lamb with remaining mint, salt, pepper and garlic. Shape into 4 patties. Brush each side with oil.

Heat grill to medium. Cook patties, flipping frequently, until well browned and a meat thermometer shows internal temperature of 160°.

Garnish with avocado sauce, endive and onion.

STUFFED LAMB BURGER WITH HIDDEN DELIGHTS

You can make many delicious variations of this basic burger. Lamb is the most easily digestible of all red meats and that, along with its mild flavor, makes lamb a perfect base for all varieties of burger stuffings.

2 tbs. minced red onion, Vidalia onion, leeks or chives

1 tbs. finely chopped bell pepper, seeded jalapeños, grated turnip or carrot curls

2 tbs. finely chopped pickled beets or relish of choice

1/4 cup finely crumbled blue cheese or other cheese of choice

1 tbs. coarse-ground brown mustard or other mustard or mayonnaise of choice

1 lb. lean ground lamb

8 slices sourdough rye or bread of choice

sliced tomato, apple, green onions or cucumber for garnish

lettuce, escarole, endive, spinach, fresh parsley or watercress for garnish

In a small bowl, mix onion, bell pepper, beets, cheese and mustard. Set aside. Shape lamb into 8 thin patties. Divide cheese mixture evenly among 4 of the patties, leaving a 1/2-inch margin all around. Top with remaining 4 patties. Seal edges well with fork or fingers.

Heat grill to medium and cook patties, flipping frequently, until patties are well browned and a meat thermometer shows internal temperature of 160°. Garnish with tomato and lettuce.

LAMB BURGER WITH EGGPLANT-GARLIC SAUCE

Servings: 4

This is another healthy and hearty recipe from the Mediterranean. Look for a male eggplant with no node on the bottom: it will have no seeds!

SAUCE

1 medium eggplant, pierced all around
2 small carrots, grated
3 cloves garlic, minced
1 tsp. Louisiana hot sauce
$\frac{1}{2}$ cup chopped fresh cilantro or watercress
3 green onions, including tops, chopped
1 tbs. cider vinegar
1 tbs. fresh lemon juice
$\frac{1}{4}$ cup extra-virgin olive oil

BURGERS

$1\frac{1}{2}$ lb. lean ground lamb
4 large pita pocket breads

Heat oven to 400°. Place eggplant on foil and roast in oven for about 30 minutes, or until soft. Quarter lengthwise and set aside to cool. Mix carrots, garlic, hot sauce, cilantro and onions and then whisk in vinegar, lemon juice and oil until mixture has the consistency of a paste. Scoop eggplant from skin, discarding skin. Add eggplant and paste mixture to a blender container, a ¼ of each at a time, and blend on slow. Drizzle oil into blender container while blending. Set aside.

Shape lamb into 4 patties. Heat grill to medium. Cook patties, flipping frequently, until well browned and a meat thermometer shows internal temperature of 160°. Garnish with eggplant sauce.

GOLD MEDAL YOGURT LAMB BURGER

If available, cherry tomatoes are another suitable garnish for this dish.

1 pkg. (1 oz.) dry ranch dip or dressing mix
2 cups plain yogurt, divided
2 small cucumbers, peeled, seeded and diced
2 green onions, including tops, finely
  chopped, divided

2 lb. ground lamb
8 pita bread pockets, 6 inches in diameter
chopped fresh cilantro for garnish

In a large bowl, stir together dip mix with 1½ cups of the yogurt. Remove ¾ cup of the yogurt mixture to a small bowl, leaving remainder in the large bowl.

To small bowl, add remaining yogurt, cucumbers and onions. Mix well, cover and refrigerate.

To large bowl, add lamb, combine well and shape into 8 patties.

Spray cold grill with nonstick cooking spray and heat to medium. Cook patties, flipping frequently, until well browned and a meat thermometer shows internal temperature of 160°.

Serve with cucumber-yogurt mixture and garnish with cilantro.

CHICKEN AND TURKEY BURGERS

COMFORT ME WITH APPLES BURGER

These are true "comfort" burgers with a pleasant aroma, civilized taste, smooth texture and satisfying substance. They're also easy and economical to make and low in calories and fats.

1 small apple, peeled and diced
1 cup finely chopped fresh mushrooms
3 cloves garlic, minced
1 cup nonfat chicken broth
1/4 pkg. (5 1/4 oz. pkg.) tabbouleh mix, with 1/2 tsp. seasoning from packet
1 lb. ground skinless chicken or turkey breast
2 green onions, including tops, chopped
2 tbs. tamari or soy sauce
2 tbs. black pepper
2 tbs. extra-virgin olive oil
4 large crusty hard rolls
sautéed Vidalia onions for garnish

In a medium saucepan over medium-high heat, place apple, mushrooms, garlic and broth and bring to a boil. Add tabbouleh and seasoning to saucepan and bring to a boil. Reduce heat to low and simmer until liquid is absorbed. Cool slightly.

Transfer mixture to a large bowl and add chicken, onions, tamari and pepper. Shape into 4 patties. Brush each side with olive oil.

Spray cold grill with nonstick cooking spray and heat to medium. Cook patties, flipping frequently, until well browned and a meat thermometer shows internal temperature of 180°.

Toast rolls on grill. Garnish with sautéed onion.

FLAMENCO BURGER CON SALSA INSOLENTE

Servings: 4

Flamenco is the thunderously stomping Spanish dance; salsa is sauce; insolente is just what you think it is. Since saffron is expensive, you could use turmeric instead.

SALSA

1/2 tbs. Worcestershire sauce
1 tbs. cider vinegar
1 tbs. extra-virgin olive oil
1/4 tsp. salt
1 tbs. dehydrated garlic
2 tbs. each black pepper and dried oregano

1 tbs. ground cumin
1 tbs. seeded, minced jalapeño chile
1 tbs. red onion, minced
1 cup chopped tomato
1/2 cup chopped cucumber
1/4 cup cooked, pureed beet

BURGERS

1 lb. ground skinless chicken or turkey thighs
1/2 lb. lean ground pork tenderloin
1/2 cup crushed whole wheat saltine crackers
1/2 tsp. lemon zest
1 tsp. black pepper

1/8 tsp. saffron threads, or 1/2 tsp. turmeric
16 small shrimp, peeled and deveined
3 tbs. extra-virgin olive oil
4 large crusty rolls, split in half
escarole for garnish

In a small bowl, combine all salsa ingredients and mix well. Set aside.

In a large bowl, combine chicken, pork, crackers, lemon zest and pepper. Crumble saffron over mixture and combine well. Shape into 8 thin patties. Press 4 shrimp each into the tops of 4 of the patties. Top with remaining 4 patties and seal edges well with fork or fingers. Brush each side with oil.

Heat grill to medium. Cook patties, flipping frequently, until well browned and a meat thermometer shows an interior temperature of 180°. Toast rolls on grill. Serve with salsa and garnish with escarole.

TRANSYLVANIAN TURKEY GARLIC BURGER

Several centuries ago, there really was a Count Dracula; his name was Vlad the Impaler. He was a ruthless leader, and garlic probably didn't do much to stop him. Today, however, garlic does help to ward off cancer and high blood pressure. Best of all, it tastes great.

1 lb. lean ground skinless turkey thigh, beef or lamb
¼ cup grated romano cheese
2 cloves garlic, minced
1 tsp. extra-virgin olive oil
1 tsp. low-sodium soy sauce
1 tbs. black pepper
8 slices tomato-basil bread or any bread
Dijon mustard, chopped fresh basil, sliced Swiss cheese
   and sliced tomato for garnish

In a medium bowl, combine meat, cheese, garlic, olive oil, soy sauce and pepper. Shape into 4 patties. Heat grill to medium. Cook patties, flipping frequently, until well browned and a meat thermometer shows internal temperature of 180°. Toast bread on grill. Garnish with mustard, basil, cheese and tomato.

GRAN'S TURK BURGER WITH OATMEAL

Despite the number of times I broke her bedroom window as a child, my Gran always fed me very well. This is her wonderful, hearty turkey burger recipe.

1/2 cup coarsely chopped yellow onion
1/2 cup coarsely chopped green bell pepper
1 lb. ground skinless turkey thigh meat
1/4 cup coarse brown mustard
1 large egg, well beaten
1/3 cup uncooked oatmeal

1/3 cup low-sodium soy sauce
1/2 cup chopped fresh parsley
8 slices sourdough rye bread, toasted
shredded low-fat mozzarella cheese for
  garnish

Place onion and bell pepper in a microwave-proof dish and microwave 3 to 4 minutes on high, or until tender. Set aside.

In a large bowl, combine turkey, mustard, egg, oatmeal, soy sauce and parsley. Shape into 4 patties.

Spray cold grill with nonstick cooking spray and heat to medium. Cook patties, flipping frequently, until well browned and a meat thermometer shows internal temperature of 180°. Garnish with onion, bell pepper and mozzarella.

DOUBLE STUFFED TURKEY BURGER

Though skinless turkey breast is very low-fat, these burgers are hearty enough to be a hit with lumberjacks. Make two of the burgers stuffed with cranberry sauce and cheddar and two stuffed with peppers, onions, mushrooms and blue cheese.

1½ lb. ground skinless turkey breast

STUFFING 1:

4 slices extra-sharp cheddar cheese
Black pepper to taste

2 tbs. whole-berry cranberry sauce

STUFFING 2:

¼ cup finely chopped yellow onion
¼ green bell pepper, finely chopped
½ cup thinly sliced fresh mushrooms

2 tbs. crumbled blue cheese
¼ cup barbecue sauce
4 large kaiser rolls, sliced and toasted

Shape turkey into 8 thin patties.

Place a slice of cheese on each of 2 patties, leaving a ½-inch margin all around. Sprinkle cheese with black pepper. Spread cranberry sauce over cheese and add remaining cheese slices. Top each with a patty and seal edges well with fork or fingers.

In a microwave-proof bowl, microwave onion and bell pepper on high for 2 minutes, until tender. Add mushrooms and cheese. Divide mixture between 2 of the patties, leaving a ½-inch margin all around. Top with remaining 2 patties and seal edges well with fork or fingers.

Heat grill to medium. Cook all patties, flipping frequently, until well browned and a meat thermometer shows internal temperature of 180°. Brush tops of burgers with barbecue sauce and grill for 2 minutes, until sauce begins to glaze.

PRETZELED POULTRY BURGER

If possible, don't buy ground chicken or turkey off the supermarket shelf; instead buy fresh breast and thighs and ask the butcher to remove the skin and bone and grind the meat. That way you get the freshest, purest meat possible.

2/3 cup finely crushed pretzels
1/3 cup finely chopped yellow onion
1/2 cup finely chopped celery
2 tbs. dried parsley
1 tsp. dried oregano
1 tsp. black pepper
1 large egg, lightly beaten

1 tbs. soy sauce
1 dash Tabasco sauce
1 1/2 lb. ground chicken or turkey
2 tbs. extra-virgin olive oil
6 large whole wheat rolls, split and toasted
sliced tomatoes and escarole for garnish

In a large bowl, combine pretzels, onion, celery, parsley, oregano, pepper, egg, soy sauce, Tabasco and chicken. Shape into 6 patties.

In a large skillet over medium heat, heat oil and cook patties, flipping frequently, until well browned on each side and a meat thermometer shows internal temperature of 180°. Serve on toasted rolls. Garnish with tomatoes and escarole.

TURKEY BURGER A LA CASBAH

Pico de gallo is a relish of finely chopped jicama, oranges, onions, bell peppers, jalapeños, cucumbers and seasonings. Cinnamon helps give this burger its North African 'Casbah' flavor.

1 medium red onion, chopped
1/2 cup pico de gallo or other medium salsa
1/2 cup pitted chopped green olives
1/2 cup dried red currants
1 tsp. grated lemon zest
1/2 tsp. each cinnamon and black pepper

1/2 tsp. ground cumin
1 tsp. sesame seeds
1 1/2 lb. skinless ground dark meat turkey
3 tbs. extra-virgin olive oil
6 large crusty sesame seed rolls, split
escarole and sliced tomato for garnish

In a large bowl, combine onion, salsa, olives, currants, lemon zest, cinnamon, pepper, cumin, sesame seeds and turkey. Shape mixture into 6 patties. Brush patties on each side with oil.

Heat grill to medium. Cook, flipping frequently, until patties are well browned and a meat thermometer shows internal temperature of 180°. Serve on toasted rolls and garnish with escarole and tomato.

TURKEY WINE BURGER

Turkey breast can be very dry, but here's a sauce to help make it moist and tasty. Ask your butcher to grind fresh skinless, boneless turkey breast for you.

3 tbs. extra-virgin olive oil, divided
2 green onions, including tops, chopped
2 garlic cloves, minced
1 tbs. country-style brown mustard
$\frac{1}{2}$ tsp. dried oregano
$\frac{1}{2}$ tsp. dried dill
$\frac{1}{2}$ tsp. dried rosemary
1 tsp. cracked peppercorns
1 cup merlot or other red wine
$1\frac{1}{2}$ lb. ground turkey breast
4 thick sourdough rye rolls, split and toasted
sliced sweet onion for garnish

In a medium saucepan over medium-high heat, heat 2 tbs. of the oil. Cook onions and garlic, stirring frequently, for 2 to 3 minutes, until onions' white parts are transparent.

Add mustard, oregano, dill, rosemary and peppercorns and cook for 1 minute, stirring frequently.

Add wine, increase heat to high and cook, stirring occasionally, until sauce is reduced by about half. Reduce heat to low and cover.

Shape turkey into 4 patties. In a medium skillet over medium heat, heat remaining oil and cook burgers, flipping frequently, until well browned and a meat thermometer shows internal temperature of 180°. Serve on toasted sourdough rye rolls. Garnish with wine sauce and onion.

TWO-TONE GINGER CHICKEN BURGER

Servings: 4

The light and dark meat make this burger juicier and more flavorful than white meat alone. The ginger gives it an exotic, Eastern taste.

1¼ lb. ground chicken or turkey, half dark meat, half white meat
2 tbs. grated fresh ginger
2 tbs. finely chopped green bell pepper
2 tbs. low-sodium soy sauce
2 tbs. Worcestershire sauce
2 cloves garlic, minced
⅓ cup finely chopped yellow onion
⅓ cup chopped fresh parsley, packed
1 tsp. black pepper
2 tbs. extra-virgin olive oil
4 kaiser rolls, split and toasted
bean or alfalfa sprouts for garnish

In a large bowl, combine chicken, ginger, bell pepper, soy sauce, Worcestershire, garlic, onion, parsley and black pepper.

Shape into 4 patties. In a large skillet over medium heat, heat oil and cook patties, flipping frequently, until well browned and a meat thermometer shows internal temperature of 180°. Serve on rolls; garnish with sprouts.

CRANBERRIED TURKEY BURGER

These burgers make a fun alternative dish for a low-key thanksgiving feast, but you can feel comfortable serving them at any time of year. Cranberry is traditional with turkey, but of course goes very well with chicken also.

1½ lb. boneless, skinless turkey or chicken breast, cut into chunks
1 large yellow onion, chopped
1 tbs. black pepper
⅛ tsp. cayenne pepper
1 tsp. dried sage
¼ cup sharp brown mustard
8 slices pesto bread
whole-berry cranberry sauce and escarole for garnish

In a food processor workbowl, place turkey, onion, black and cayenne peppers, sage and mustard and chop finely. Shape mixture into 4 patties.

Spray cold grill with nonstick cooking spray and heat to medium. Cook patties, flipping frequently, until well browned and a meat thermometer shows internal temperature of 180°. Toast bread slices on grill. Garnish with cranberry sauce and escarole.

VEGETARIAN, TOFU AND FISH BURGERS

NUTTY TOFU BURGER

If meat isn't on the menu, you can still satisfy your appetite for protein with these burgers.

1 lb. firm tofu, pressed dry between paper
   towels
2 tbs. extra-virgin olive oil, divided
1 large yellow onion, finely chopped
2 large cloves garlic, minced
1 tsp. dried thyme
1 tsp. dried dill
1 tbs. soy sauce
1 tsp. Worcestershire sauce

3 cups finely chopped mushrooms
1 tsp. curry powder
1 1/2 cups cooked rice
1/4 cup finely chopped Brazil nuts
2 tsp. Dijon mustard
1/3 tsp. black pepper
2 small eggs, lightly beaten
6 pita bread pockets
sliced tomatoes for garnish

In a large bowl, mash tofu and set aside. In a large nonstick skillet over medium-high heat, place 1 tbs. of the oil, onion, garlic, thyme and dill and cook for about 5 minutes, or until onion is translucent. Add soy sauce, Worcestershire, mushrooms and curry powder and cook for about 8 minutes, until lightly browned. Add to bowl with tofu. Stir in rice, nuts, mustard, pepper and eggs and combine well. Shape into 6 patties. In a skillet over medium-high heat, heat remaining oil. Add patties and cook for 3 to 4 minutes per side, or until well browned. Garnish with tomato.

BULGUR AND BEAN BURGER

These tasty burgers are a vegetarian treat.

1 medium yellow squash, chopped
½ cup plain yogurt
1 tbs. red wine vinegar
1 cup chopped fresh dill, divided
1 cup uncooked bulgur wheat
2 tbs. fresh lemon juice with pulp
1 cup chopped fresh parsley
¼ cup canola oil, divided
3 cloves garlic, minced
⅓ cup finely chopped green onions, including tops

3 tbs. finely chopped pistachios
2 tsp. ground coriander
2 tsp. ground cumin
½ tsp. red pepper flakes
1 can (15 oz.) garbanzo beans, drained
2½ tbs. all-purpose flour
3 large egg whites
6 crusty rolls, or 12 slices bread

In a small bowl, combine squash, yogurt, vinegar and $1/2$ cup of the dill. Cover and refrigerate.

In a medium saucepan over high heat, bring $3/4$ cup water to a boil. Add bulgur and lemon juice. Remove from heat, cover and let stand for 30 minutes, until liquid is absorbed. Stir in parsley.

In a large skillet over medium heat, heat 1 tbs. of the oil. Add garlic, onions, pistachios, coriander, cumin, remaining dill and pepper flakes. Cook, stirring frequently, until white parts of onions are translucent.

In a blender container or food processor workbowl, place 1 tbs. of the oil and garbanzos and process until smooth. In a large bowl, combine garbanzos and onion mixture with bulgur mixture, flour and egg whites. Shape mixture into 6 patties. In a large skillet over medium heat, place remaining 2 tbs. oil and cook patties for about 4 minutes until browned, then flip and cook for 2 to 3 minutes longer. Garnish with squash sauce and serve on rolls or bread.

HEAVENLY LENTIL AND SPICE BURGER

These burgers contain lots of nutritious complex carbohydrates. If you're into marathons, English Channel swimming, or are a mother with small children, these will give you the stamina you need.

½ cup dry lentils
½ lb. small red potatoes, cut into ½-inch
   cubes
½ cup chopped cauliflower
½ cup thinly sliced carrots
½ cup frozen young peas, thawed
2 tbs. canola oil, divided
½ yellow onion, minced
1 clove garlic, minced
¼ tsp. dry mustard

¼ tsp. red pepper flakes
¼ tsp. ground cumin
½ tsp. curry
2 tbs. finely chopped fresh cilantro
¼ cup uncooked instant Cream of Wheat or
   instant hominy grits
⅓ cup egg substitute
½ cup fine dry breadcrumbs
6 pita pocket breads

In a medium saucepan over high heat, cover lentils with water and bring to a boil. Reduce heat to low, cover and simmer for 30 minutes until tender. Drain, mash and set aside.

In a medium saucepan over high heat, bring 1 cup water to a boil. Add potatoes, cauliflower, carrots and peas and boil for 1 minute. Drain and set aside.

In a large skillet over medium heat, heat 1 tbs. of the oil. Add onion, garlic, mustard, pepper flakes, cumin and curry and cook for 5 minutes, stirring frequently, until onion is translucent. Remove from heat and stir in cilantro.

In a large bowl, combine lentils, potato-vegetable and onion mixtures with Cream of Wheat and shape into 6 patties. Pour egg substitute and breadcrumbs onto separate plates. Dip each side of each patty in egg substitute, then in breadcrumbs. Place oil in skillet over medium heat and cook patties for 5 to 6 minutes, until browned. Serve in pita pockets.

RED-LETTER LENTIL BURGER

These French-style burgers are vegetarian, yet are high in protein and essential nutrients. They are also low in calories and fat. Voila!

1/3 cup mayonnaise
4 tsp. fresh lemon juice, divided
4 cloves garlic, minced, divided
1 cup dried red lentils
1 tsp. salt, divided
3 tbs. extra-virgin olive oil, divided
1 medium carrot, shaved into ribbons with
  vegetable peeler
1 medium yellow onion, finely chopped
1 tsp. black pepper

1 tsp. dried marjoram
2 cans (4 oz. each) sliced mushrooms, drained
1/2 cup dry sherry or white wine
1 slice pumpernickel bread, toasted and finely
  crushed
1/2 cup egg substitute, or 3 egg whites
6 large sesame seed rolls, split
lettuce, sliced onion and sliced tomato for
  garnish

In a small bowl, whisk mayonnaise, 1 tsp. of the lemon juice and 1 clove of the garlic. Cover and refrigerate. In a medium saucepan over medium-high heat add 3 cups cold water, lentils and ½ tsp. of the salt. Bring to a boil, reduce heat to simmer, cover and cook for 25 minutes or until lentils are soft. Drain and set aside.

In a large skillet over medium heat, place 2 tbs. of the oil and cook remaining 3 cloves garlic, carrot and onion for 3 minutes. Add pepper, remaining ½ tsp. salt, marjoram, mushrooms and sherry and continue to cook for about 2 minutes, until liquid is reduced. Place in a large bowl to cool. To onion mixture in bowl add breadcrumbs, remaining 1 tbs. lemon juice, egg substitute and lentils. Shape mixture into 6 patties. Brush each side with remaining oil. Place in a large skillet over medium heat and cook for 5 minutes on each side, until browned. Toast rolls in skillet. Garnish with mayonnaise mixture, lettuce, onion and tomato.

EASY TUNA BURGER WITH DILL

These delicious burgers are so quick and easy, they're great for a crowd.

2 eggs
1/3 cup dry bread crumbs
1 tbs. chopped fresh dill, or 1 tsp. dried
1 tbs. horseradish sauce
2 tsp. brown mustard
black pepper to taste
salt to taste

1 can (12 oz.) water-packed tuna, drained
2 green onions, minced
1 celery stalk, chopped
1 tbs. vegetable oil
4 whole wheat rolls, split and toasted
lettuce leaves and tomato slices for garnish

In a medium bowl, lightly beat eggs. Mix in breadcrumbs, dill, horseradish, mustard, pepper and salt.

Add tuna , onions and celery to mixture. Shape into four 1/2-inch-thick patties.

In a nonstick skillet over medium heat, heat oil. Cook patties for about 6 minutes. Flip and cook another 4 minutes, or until golden brown and set.

Serve on toasted rolls. Garnish with lettuce and tomato.

SALMON BURGER WITH RED ONION

Servings: 8

Canned pink salmon is very inexpensive and makes burgers you'll be proud to serve to family and friends.

2 cans (15 oz. each) pink salmon, undrained
2 large eggs, lightly beaten
3/4 cup finely chopped green bell pepper
3/4 cup chopped red onion
1 cup fresh whole wheat breadcrumbs
1 tbs. grated fresh lemon zest
1 tbs. fresh lemon juice

1/4 cup Italian salad dressing, divided
1 tbs. black pepper
1 tsp. finely chopped dried rosemary
8 English muffins, split and toasted
sliced onion, sliced tomato, sprouts and lettuce
    for garnish

Place salmon in a large bowl. Discard skin and bone and mash salmon with a fork. Add eggs, bell pepper, onion, breadcrumbs, lemon zest, juice, 2 tbs. of the dressing, black pepper and rosemary. Combine well and shape into 8 patties. Drizzle 1 tbs. of the dressing evenly over patties.

In a large nonstick skillet over medium-low heat, cook patties, dressing-side down, for about 10 minutes, or until browned. Flip patties. Drizzle remaining 1 tbs. Italian dressing evenly over patties and cook for 5 to 6 minutes.

Serve on muffins; garnish with onion, tomato, sprouts and lettuce.

TOFU BURGER WITH FLAVORED MAYONNAISE

Servings: 4

Tofu is rich in nutrients and absorbs the flavors of spices, sauces and vegetables very well. This easy sauce provides a smooth complement to the hearty burgers.

SAUCE

3 tbs. mayonnaise
2 tbs. finely chopped green onion tops
1 clove garlic, minced
1 tbs. Worcestershire sauce

BURGERS

2 tbs. extra-virgin olive oil, divided
1 lb. firm tofu
1 cup cooked bulgur wheat
$\frac{1}{3}$ cup grated romano cheese
$\frac{1}{2}$ tsp. black pepper
1 tsp. dried marjoram
1 tsp. dried basil
1 tsp. dried thyme
$\frac{1}{3}$ cup skim milk
1 pinch salt
2 eggs, well beaten
$\frac{1}{4}$ cup unbleached flour
4 large, crusty hard rolls, split and toasted
lettuce, sliced tomatoes and sliced Vidalia
    onion for garnish

Combine mayonnaise, green onions, garlic and Worcestershire sauce in a small bowl. Cover and refrigerate.

Slice tofu crosswise into 4 slices and press dry between paper towels. In a large skillet over medium heat, heat 1 tbs. of the oil and cook tofu for 5 minutes on each side, or until browned.

In a small bowl, combine bulgur, cheese, pepper, marjoram, basil and thyme. In a separate bowl combine milk, salt and eggs. Put flour on a plate. Dredge tofu slices in flour; dip in egg mixture; then dip in bulgur mixture, pressing lightly.

In a skillet over medium-high heat, place remaining 1 tbs. oil and cook tofu slices for 2 minutes on each side, or until bulgur-cheese mixture is lightly browned. Serve on rolls; garnish with refrigerated sauce, lettuce, tomato and onion.

TOFU ORIENTAL BURGER WITH TAHINI

The combination of sesame seeds, sesame oil and soy sauce gives these burgers a distinctive Asian flavor.

1 lb. firm tofu, pressed dry between paper towels
2 tbs. extra-virgin olive oil, divided
2 tsp. minced fresh ginger
2/3 cup finely chopped green onions, including tops
1 clove garlic, minced
1 medium carrot, grated
1 large egg, lightly beaten
2/3 cup finely chopped toasted almonds
1 tsp. toasted sesame seeds
1 tsp. sesame oil
1 tbs. soy sauce
4 large sesame seed rolls, split and toasted
tahini (sesame seed paste), sliced tomatoes and mustard greens for garnish

In a large skillet over medium-high heat, heat 1 tbs. of the olive oil. Add ginger, onion, garlic and carrot and cook for about 3 minutes, or until white portions of onion are translucent. Cool slightly.

Place tofu in a medium bowl and mash. Add onion mixture, egg, almonds, sesame seeds, sesame oil and soy sauce. Mix well and shape into 4 patties.

Heat remaining 1 tbs. oil in a skillet over medium heat and cook patties for about 5 minutes, or until browned. Flip and cook for about 3 minutes. Serve on sesame seed rolls; garnish with tahini, tomato and greens.

ORIENT EXPRESS

COWBOY TOFU SPINACH BURGER

Today's cowboys are not the hairy, unwashed illiterates of the Old West. They now ride in air-conditioned Broncos, carry cellular phones instead of Colt .45s and are more likely to drink Perrier than Ol' Red-Eye. Watch these contemporary cowboys belly-up to these low calorie, low-fat tofu burgers. And join the roundup!

1 pkg. (10 oz.) frozen chopped spinach, thawed and drained
1 lb. firm tofu, cut into chunks
2 cups finely crushed matzos or cracker crumbs
3/4 cup minced yellow onion
2 green onions, including tops, thinly sliced
2 cloves garlic, minced
2–3 dashes Louisiana hot sauce
1 tbs. dried tarragon
1 tbs. black pepper
1 tsp. dried thyme
1 tbs. extra-virgin olive oil
1 cup shredded extra-sharp cheddar cheese
8 whole wheat rolls, split and toasted

In a food processor workbowl or blender container, add spinach, tofu, matzos, onion, green onion, garlic, hot sauce, tarragon, pepper and thyme and blend. Shape mixture into 8 patties.

In a large skillet over medium heat, add oil and cook patties for 5 minutes, until lightly browned. Flip and cook for 3 to 5 minutes longer.

Sprinkle cheese evenly over patties and cook until cheese melts. Serve on toasted rolls.

GARDEN VEGETABLE TOFU BURGER

The versatile soybean is used to make plastics and environmentally-friendly inks; is the only plant to provide all essential amino acids; is found in foods from flour to soy sauce, tofu to textured meat substitutes; and can help prevent cancer and reduce cholesterol.

1 lb. firm tofu
1/4 cup grated turnip or carrot
1 tbs. canola oil, divided
1/4 cup dark miso
1/4 cup cold water
2 cups sliced fresh mushrooms
1/2 cup diced yellow onion
1 cup diced green bell peppers
3 cloves garlic, minced

1 tbs. chopped fresh basil
1/2 cup dry white wine
1 can (6 oz.) tomato puree
1 can (14 1/2 oz.) Italian-style tomatoes
8 slices sourdough rye bread
chopped fresh cilantro or parsley and minced
   chiles for garnish

In a medium bowl, mash tofu and combine with turnip. Shape into 4 patties. Brush patties on both sides with 1 tsp. of the oil. Cover with foil and refrigerate.

In a small bowl, dissolve miso in water. Set aside.

In a medium saucepan over medium-high heat, heat 1 tsp. of the oil and cook mushrooms, onion, bell pepper and garlic for 4 to 5 minutes, until onion is lightly browned. Reduce heat to low. Add basil, miso dissolved in water, wine, puree and tomatoes. Simmer uncovered for 10 to 12 minutes.

In a large skillet over medium-high heat, heat remaining 1 tsp. oil and cook patties for about 6 minutes. Flip and cook for about 4 minutes, until patties are browned. Reduce heat to low, top burgers with sauce and simmer uncovered for 5 minutes.

Toast bread if desired; garnish with cilantro and chiles.

MUSHROOM BURGER FOR CARNIVORES

Mushrooms, cilantro and roasted red peppers combine to make a "meaty" vegetarian burger that satisfies.

4 very large portobello mushroom caps
2 tbs. extra-virgin olive oil
1 cup sliced red bell peppers
4 slices fontina or similar cheese

2 cups chopped fresh cilantro, watercress or
  parsley
8 slices sourdough bread
sliced black olives for garnish

Spray cold grill with nonstick cooking spray and heat to medium-high. Rub mushrooms with oil, place top- (dome) side up on grill and cook for 4 to 5 minutes, or until mushrooms begin to drip.

While mushrooms are cooking, place bell pepper in a microwave-safe bowl and microwave on high for 2 to 3 minutes, or until crisp-tender. Turn mushrooms bottom- (gill) side up. Spread pepper slices evenly over mushrooms and cover with cheese. Cook for about 2 minutes, or until cheese begins to melt. Sprinkle evenly with cilantro and cook for 1 minute.

Toast bread slices on grill. Garnish with olives.

BLACK BEAN BURGER

Black beans, also called turtle beans, have a sweet and rich flavor that forms an excellent base for these delicious burgers.

3 cans (16 oz. each) black beans, rinsed,
    drained and mashed
1½ cups uncooked regular oatmeal
1 large yellow onion, finely chopped
2 jalapeño chiles, seeded and diced
2 large eggs, well beaten

½ cup purchased waffle mix
2 tbs. canola oil
16 slices dark rye bread
sliced dill pickles, sliced tomatoes and
    horseradish for garnish

In a large bowl, combine beans, oatmeal, onion, jalapeño, eggs and waffle mix. Shape into 8 patties.

In a large skillet over medium-high heat, heat canola oil. Cook patties for 5 to 6 minutes on first side, flip and cook for 3 to 4 minutes, until well browned.

Toast bread lightly in skillet. Garnish with dill pickles, tomato and horseradish.

SAUCES

BASIC BARBECUE SAUCE

This simple sauce is very versatile; it serves to enhance flavor and to put a glaze on burgers and other grilled meats, poultry and even tofu.

1 cup sharp mustard
1 cup cider vinegar
1 cup dark molasses

Combine all ingredients in a medium bowl, stirring vigorously. Pour into sealable 1-cup plastic containers. Label, date and freeze.

Thaw at room temperature. Can be kept refrigerated for up to 30 days.

BORDELAISE SAUCE

This sauce is best on beef, buffalo and venison burgers, steak and meat loaf. This recipe can easily be doubled or halved.

1 can (6 oz.) sliced mushrooms, undrained
1 can (10½ oz.) mushroom gravy
1 tbs. finely chopped red onion
1 tbs. butter
½ tsp. dried thyme
1 bay leaf
½ cup chopped fresh parsley

In a small saucepan, combine mushrooms, gravy, onion, butter, thyme and bay leaf. Bring to a boil, reduce heat to low and simmer for 15 minutes. Remove and discard bay leaf. Stir in parsley and serve hot. Do not freeze.

BURGUNDY WINE SAUCE

This sauce goes well with almost anything, be it burger, meat loaf, steak, roast or dark meat fowl. For the best flavored sauce, avoid supermarket cooking wine — use the real stuff.

2 tbs. unsalted butter
1 tbs. finely chopped green onion, tops included
3 tbs. all-purpose flour
1/2 cup beef broth
1/2 cup burgundy or other full-bodied red wine
1 tbs. chopped fresh parsley

In a small saucepan over medium-high heat, melt butter. Add onion and cook until white portion is translucent. Add flour and cook for 1 minute. Gradually stir in broth and wine and cook until sauce begins to bubble. Stir in parsley. Serve warm. Refrigerate any surplus.

CALIFORNIA GUACAMOLE SAUCE

Thomas Jefferson knew avocados as "alligator pears" from France. He probably didn't suspect that one day most of the United States' avocados would come from California. He would have appreciated the magic this sauce works on burgers and baked potatoes. It also makes a great dip for raw vegetables (crudités).

1 avocado, mashed
1 large beefsteak tomato, chopped, drained on paper towels
$1/3$ cup mayonnaise
$1/3$ cup fresh lemon juice
$1\frac{1}{2}$ tsp. grated red onion
$1/2$ tsp. salt
1 tbs. Louisiana hot sauce

In a small bowl, combine avocado with tomato, mayonnaise, lemon juice, onion, salt and hot sauce. Cover and refrigerate. Best served within 2 to 4 hours. Refrigerate any leftovers in tightly-covered container for up to 5 days.

ALL DAY, EVERY DAY CHEDDAR SAUCE

This amazingly versatile sauce works wonderfully over eggs, burgers and meat loaf; in Reubens, BLTs and Philly cheese steak sandwiches; over broiled fish, veggies, baked potatoes, rice and pastas; and on apple pie.

1/4 cup unsalted butter
1/4 cup all-purpose flour
1 tbs. black pepper
2 1/2 cups skim milk
1 cup shredded sharp cheddar cheese
1 tbs. Worcestershire sauce

In a medium saucepan over medium heat, melt butter. Stir in flour and pepper and cook, stirring constantly, until mixture begins to bubble. Add milk and continue to stir until mixture bubbles again. Add cheese and Worcestershire sauce and stir until cheese is melted.

CREAMY MUSTARD & MAYONNAISE SAUCE

Beef, buffalo, venison, meat loaf, burgers, steaks and roasts will all seem richer and more comforting with a dollop or two of this different sauce. This recipe can easily be doubled or tripled to serve a crowd.

1/4 cup nonfat beef broth
1/2 cup mayonnaise
1/4 cup sour cream
1/4 cup brown mustard

In a small bowl combine all ingredients and mix well. Refrigerate for 15 minutes before serving. Sauce will keep in refrigerator for up to 5 days.

RED CURRANT, GINGER AND MUSTARD SAUCE

Pork, lamb, turkey and tofu burgers all become newsworthy with this colorful, tangy sauce.

2/3 cup red currant jelly
1 tbs. grated lemon zest
1 tsp. grated red onion
1 tsp. dry mustard
1/2 tsp. ground ginger
1/4 cup fresh lemon juice

In a small saucepan over medium-low heat, combine all ingredients. Stir constantly until jelly melts and sauce is well blended.

GINGER ZINFANDEL SAUCE

This is an exceptionally good ginger sauce and is great with pork, lamb and tofu burgers and on baked and broiled fish.

1 tbs. butter
3 green onions, including tops, minced
3 tbs. minced fresh ginger
1/2 cup zinfandel or other dry red wine
3/4 cup cold unsalted butter, diced
1/3 cup chopped crystallized ginger
1/4 tsp. white pepper
1/4 tsp. salt

In a large saucepan over low heat, melt butter. Add onions and ginger and cook for about 4 minutes, stirring constantly, until white parts of onion are translucent. Increase heat to medium-high, add wine and boil for 4 minutes, or until mixture is reduced by about 1/4. Pour through a fine sieve into a bowl and discard solids. Return mixture to saucepan and reduce heat to low. Whisk in diced butter gradually and continue whisking until sauce is creamy. Do not allow sauce to boil. Stir in crystallized ginger, pepper and salt. Serve sauce at once, while still warm.

MINTY ORANGE SAUCE

Lamb, pork and turkey all take on new personalities with this sauce. As a matter of fact, so do fish and tofu. And you'll never think of Spam the same way again.

1/2 cup orange marmalade
1/4 cup yellow mustard
1/4 cup chopped fresh mint

In a small saucepan over low heat, combine marmalade and mustard. Stir occasionally until marmalade is melted. Stir in mint. Serve warm or cold.

SPICY PLUM SAUCE

Here's a sauce that's both sweet and sharp. In the burger realm, it stars on pork, lamb, turkey and tofu, and has the winning formula for any number of Chinese dishes, from egg rolls to tea-smoked duck.

1 cup plum jam
1 tsp. grated red onion
1 tbs. cider vinegar
½ tsp. ground allspice
½ tsp. ground ginger
¼ tsp. cayenne pepper

In a small saucepan over medium heat, combine all ingredients and cook, stirring constantly, until mixture begins to boil. Remove from heat and allow to cool to room temperature. Chill before using. Sauce will keep, tightly sealed, for up to 30 days in the refrigerator.

SOUR CREAM RADISH SAUCE

There are red, pink, white, purple, green and black radishes — have fun experimenting with the possibilities. This sauce adds a crisp zing to burgers, baked potatoes and even white rice.

1 cup sour cream
1 cup finely chopped radishes
$1/4$ cup finely chopped fresh chives
1 tbs. black pepper
$1/2$ tsp. salt

In a small bowl, blend all ingredients well. Cover and refrigerate until ready to serve. Sauce will keep for up to a week in the refrigerator.

ROQUEFORT CHEESE & SHERRY SAUCE

Beef, buffalo and venison; roast duck and goose; most fish; most veggies; shirred and fried eggs; croissants; crepes; waffles and even bagels ... all assume new and improved character traits with this elegant sauce.

$1/2$ cup Roquefort or blue cheese, softened
$1/4$ cup butter, softened
$1/4$ cup dry sherry
1 tsp. black pepper

In a small bowl, mash cheese and butter together with a fork. Add sherry and pepper and beat until smooth. May be refrigerated, but bring to room temperature before using.

SALSA DIABLO

This is a South-of-the-Border approach to the basic barbecue sauce and works best on grilled beef and buffalo burgers and steaks. If you're adventurous, also try it on pork chops and hot dogs.

½ cup dark molasses
½ cup cider vinegar
¾ cup sharp mustard
½ tsp. Tabasco sauce
1 tbs. Worcestershire sauce

In a medium bowl, combine all ingredients, stirring vigorously to mix. Pour in sealable cup-sized plastic containers; label, date and freeze. Or, sauce can be refrigerated for up to 30 days.

VOODOO CHILE SAUCE

Despite this sauce's serious heat, it won't really raise the dead ... but it'll put real life into anything in need of extra zing. I think it goes best with pork burgers, but it's also magical on tofu and bean burgers, pork, shrimp, oysters and eggs. Serious chile heads can substitute serranos or scotch bonnets for the jalapeños.

3 cloves garlic, peeled
2 small jalapeño chiles, seeded
1 tsp. lightly toasted whole cumin seeds
1 tsp. sea salt
1 tsp. black pepper

½ cup extra-virgin olive oil
¼ cup fresh pink grapefruit juice with pulp
1 tsp. dry sherry
1 dash Angostura Bitters

In a blender container or food processor workbowl, puree garlic, chiles, cumin, salt and pepper. Leave in blender container.

In a small saucepan over medium-high, heat oil for about 3 minutes or until hot. Pour over chile mixture in blender container and pulse 2 or 3 times to mix well. Add juice, sherry and bitters and pulse 2 or 3 times. Refrigerate any leftover sauce in a sealed container.

INDEX

O

Oatmeal with Gran's turk burger 75
Onion, red with salmon burger 93
Onions with beef burger 21
Orange minty sauce 113

P

Pepper and beef all-American burger 14
Picante beef burger 42
Pickle-dilly circus beef burger 38
Pico de gallo relish, in turkey burger a la Casbah 79
Pine nuts and fontina with Sicilian beef burger 35
Pineapple and guacamole with Aloha burger 16
Pineapple in Hawaiian-style pork or lamb burger 58
Plum sauce, spicy 114
Pork
   chipotle and adobo burger 56
   or lamb Hawaiian-style burger 58
   wet Wednesday burger 55

Portobello in mushroom burger for carnivores 102
Portobello stacked burger 44
Poultry burger, pretzeled 78
Pretzeled poultry burger 78

R

Radish and sour cream sauce 115
Red currant, ginger and mustard sauce 111
Roquefort cheese and sherry sauce 116
Runza midwestern beef burger 40

S

Salmon burger with red onion 93
Salsa diablo 117
Salsa insolente with flamenco burger 72
Sauce(s)
   all day, every day cheddar 109
   basic barbecue 105
   Bordelaise 106
   Burgundy wine 107

California guacamole 108
commercial barbecue 8
creamy mustard and mayonnaise 110
cucumber, with Corfu lamb burger 62
ginger zinfandel 112
minty orange 113
red currant, ginger and mustard 111
Roquefort cheese and sherry 116
salsa diablo 117
sour cream radish 115
spicy plum 114
voodoo chile 118
Saucily-minted lamb burger 64
Sausage, Polish in Zella's mixed grill burger 47
Sherry and Roquefort cheese sauce 116
Sloppy joe in easy spoon-on burger 28
Smoked cheese, chipotle and bacon burger 29
Sour cream radish sauce 115

Serve Creative, Easy, Nutritious Meals with nitty gritty® Cookbooks

100 Dynamite Desserts
The 9 x 13 Pan Cookbook
The Barbecue Cookbook
Beer and Good Food
The Best Bagels are Made at Home
The Best Pizza is Made at Home
The Big Book of Bread Machine Recipes
Blender Drinks
Bread Baking
Bread Machine Cookbook
Bread Machine Cookbook II
Bread Machine Cookbook III
Bread Machine Cookbook IV
Bread Machine Cookbook V
Bread Machine Cookbook VI
The Little Burger Bible
Cappuccino/Espresso
Casseroles
The Coffee Book
Convection Oven Cookery
The Cook-Ahead Cookbook
Cooking for 1 or 2
Cooking in Clay

Cooking in Porcelain
Cooking on the Indoor Grill
Cooking with Chile Peppers
Cooking with Grains
Cooking with Your Kids
The Dehydrator Cookbook
Edible Pockets for Every Meal
Entrees from Your Bread Machine
Extra-Special Crockery Pot Recipes
Fabulous Fiber Cookery
Fondue and Hot Dips
Fresh Vegetables
From Freezer, 'Fridge and Pantry
From Your Ice Cream Maker
The Garlic Cookbook
Gourmet Gifts
Healthy Cooking on the Run
Healthy Snacks for Kids
The Juicer Book
The Juicer Book II
Lowfat American Favorites
New International Fondue Cookbook
No Salt, No Sugar, No Fat

One-Dish Meals
The Pasta Machine Cookbook
Pinch of Time: Meals in Less than 30
    Minutes
Quick and Easy Pasta Recipes
Recipes for the Loaf Pan
Recipes for the Pressure Cooker
Recipes for Yogurt Cheese
Risottos, Paellas, and other Rice
    Specialties
Rotisserie Oven Cooking
The Sandwich Maker Cookbook
The Sensational Skillet: Sautés and Stir-Fries
Slow Cooking in Crock-Pot,® Slow Cooker,
    Oven and Multi-Cooker
Soups and Stews
The Toaster Oven Cookbook
Unbeatable Chicken Recipes
The Vegetarian Slow Cooker
New Waffles and Pizzelles
Wraps and Roll-Ups

For a free catalog, call: Bristol Publishing Enterprises, Inc.
(800) 346-4889
www.bristolcookbooks.com